YOUR KNOWLEDGE HAS VALUE

- We will publish your bachelor's and master's thesis, essays and papers

- Your own eBook and book - sold worldwide in all relevant shops

- Earn money with each sale

Upload your text at www.GRIN.com
and publish for free

Bibliographic information published by the German National Library:

The German National Library lists this publication in the National Bibliography; detailed bibliographic data are available on the Internet at http://dnb.dnb.de .

This book is copyright material and must not be copied, reproduced, transferred, distributed, leased, licensed or publicly performed or used in any way except as specifically permitted in writing by the publishers, as allowed under the terms and conditions under which it was purchased or as strictly permitted by applicable copyright law. Any unauthorized distribution or use of this text may be a direct infringement of the author s and publisher s rights and those responsible may be liable in law accordingly.

Imprint:

Copyright © 2015 GRIN Verlag, Open Publishing GmbH
Print and binding: Books on Demand GmbH, Norderstedt Germany
ISBN: 9783668589353

This book at GRIN:

http://www.grin.com/en/e-book/382972/diversity-at-abercrombie-fitch

Marina H.

Diversity at Abercrombie & Fitch

GRIN Publishing

GRIN - Your knowledge has value

Since its foundation in 1998, GRIN has specialized in publishing academic texts by students, college teachers and other academics as e-book and printed book. The website www.grin.com is an ideal platform for presenting term papers, final papers, scientific essays, dissertations and specialist books.

Visit us on the internet:

http://www.grin.com/

http://www.facebook.com/grincom

http://www.twitter.com/grin_com

BMG570 Managing Equality & Diversity
Submission Date: 22.03.2015

Diversity at Abercrombie & Fitch

Diversity at Abercrombie & Fitch

I. Content

1. Introduction 3
2. Policy 3
    2.1 Diversity policies and the role of social justice and the business case 3
    2.2 Abercrombie & Fitch´s Diversity Policy 4
3. Abercrombie & Fitch´s Diversity in practice 4
    3.1 Race Discrimination claims 5
        3.1.1 Terms of descent decree 6
    3.2 Disability Discrimination claims 6
    3.3 Religious Discrimination claims 7
4. Current status 7
5. Conclusion 8

II. References
III. Bibliography

1. Introduction

In order to avoid discrimination and promote equality in the working environment, certain characteristics, such as gender, religion, age, disability and race are protected by law (Kumra & Manfredi, 2012). These anti-discrimination laws are often supported on an organisational level by implementing diversity policies that illustrate how in particular the individual company strives to tackle discrimination or even how it strives to promote equality or diversity (Harvey et al., 2005).

Today, nearly two-thirds of workplaces are covered by formal-written Equal Opportunity policies (Kirton, 2010). Although they are in wide use, policies and procedures are not always followed in practice (Liff, 1999) as sometimes they are purely used as "window-dressing" (Hoque & Noon, as cited in Kirton, 2010).

Using the globally renowned fashion chain *Abercrombie & Fitch* as a case example, this report´s aim is to depict its diversity policy and to analyse how the organisation meets its policy in reality. An introduction to the main approaches of diversity policies shall be given in order to analyse Abercrombie & Fitch´s diversity policy. Next, it will analyse, how the company deals with diversity in reality. Comparing this policy with a current image of the reality, it is then discussed whether or not the policy is followed in practice.

2. Policy

2.1 Diversity policies and the role of social justice and the business case

Referring to Kirton (2010), three main approaches concerning organisational equality and diversity policies are to be distinguished: the legal case, the social justice and the business case. The author states that legal compliance as well as the social justice case are both most likely associated with traditional equal employment approaches (Kirton, 2010). The legal case is closely linked to legislation and aims to ensure that the employer stays within the law (Kirton, 2010). Equality policies that are motivated by the legal case are therefore striving to engage in employment practices and procedures, which do not discriminate or contravene with the law (Dickens cited in Bach, 2000). Social justice arguments originate in the moral argument that equality is ethically right and should be pursued for this reason (McPeake, 2015).

Proceeding on the assumption that valuing workforce diversity leads to benefits for the organisation, the business case on the other hand refers to the idea of proactively promoting difference. Therefore so-called equality champions take a step further than just complying with the law and proactively promote diversity. They would therefore express their policy arguments in the language of the benefits to the business (Kirton, 2010).

2.2 Abercrombie & Fitch´s Diversity Policy

Abercrombie & Fitch´s policy determines six key drivers for its diversity strategy: Leadership Commitment, Employee Engagement, Measurement & Accountability, Communication, Training & Education, and Policy Integration (Abercrombie & Fitch, 2010 & 2011).

Statements like "We all learn from each other´s differences", "it is [Diversity] imperative to our growth that we staff our business with diverse talent and run our business with an inclusive mind-set" (Abercrombie & Fitch, 2010 & 2011) point out that the clothier clearly associates its workforce diversity with organisational benefits. Therefore, it could be concluded that the company´s policy is clearly argued in the language in terms of the business case. A video, which is linked to diversity and inclusion, underpins this impression. The video shows numerous employees of different ethnical backgrounds, all commenting on their enthusiasm about their company´s diversity. Furthermore, the Senior Vice President of Diversity and Inclusion, Todd Corley, relates to the company´s associates as *diversity champions*. Overall, the company tries hard to create a clean image in terms of its diversity management in the public appearance that goes beyond the legal compliance and celebrates as well as actively promotes diversity.

3. Abercrombie & Fitch´s Diversity in practice

"If I exclude people- absolutely. Delighted to do so"- a statement by Michael Jeffries, the CEO of *Abercrombie & Fitch,* in 2002 (Elliott, 2015 p.188). The quote represents the brand´s exclusionary marketing strategy, trying to exclusively appeal to *young, good-looking and athletic-demographic* customers (Sondak et al., 2014). As part of their marketing strategy, *Abercrombie & Fitch* made similar demands on its shop associates, paying particular attention to youth and looks, the average staff age is 27 (Halasz et al., 2006). Selecting for beauty among its sales staff, managers were instructed to *grade* their employees based on how attractive they are. When receiving a low rating, the associate was either terminated, dropped from the sales floor and asked to work in the stockroom or asked to work night shifts (McBride, 2005).

Furthermore, the author explains that every associate received a so-called *Look Book,* a book that includes instructions of adequate haircuts and styles, and other regulations concerning jewellery, which have lead to conjectures of racial undertones. In specific, the regulations have given rise to the suspicion to prohibit styles and habits typical for people of colour (McBride, 2005).

On top of that, instances give rise to the suspicion that Abercrombie & Fitch prefers a white sales force and discriminates employees of ethnic minorities: A former shop assistant, for instance, states that employees of a habitual background other than white were mainly allocated to work night shifts or in the stockroom, a low visible part of the shop. However, the day floor staffs usually completely consist of white employees (Canas et al., 2014). This supposition is supported by a race discrimination lawsuit in 2003, which is portrayed in the next part. Furthermore, special attention will also be paid to more recent discrimination claims to gain a more topical insight into recent issues.

3.1 Race Discrimination claims

In 2003, nine adults, all from ethnic minorities, were pursuing a class action lawsuit in the United States District Court of San Francisco against Abercrombie & Fitch due to its practices that discriminate against people of colour. Specifically, six of the nine litigants claim that they were fired because of their ethnic background (Edwards, 2003). Jennifer Lu, one of the plaintiffs, for instance states that she was terminated after a corporate official of the brand visited the store, pointing to an Abercrombie poster with a white Caucasian male on it and saying: "You need to have more staff that looks like this" (Canas et al., 2014 p. 126)

Furthermore, three of the nine plaintiffs, who applied for a job, state that they were refused front-of-the-sales positions because of their ethnic backgrounds. Anthony Occampo for instance, a former employee with a Filipino background was turned down after reapplying because "there are already too many Filipinos" (Meisler, 2003 p.20).

Finally, both parties negotiated a settlement, which gave compensation costs in favour of the litigants of $40,000. Despite agreeing on paying the settlement costs, the fashion chain denied the accusations. The CEO of the company, Mike Jeffries responds to the allegations by saying that Abercrombie & Fitch has never had tolerance for discrimination and that they have settled the suit in order to avoid a long, drawn out dispute that might have been harmful for the company (Canas et al., 2014).

3.1.1 Terms of descent decree

As part of the settlement, Abercrombie and Fitch also had to agree on special procedures, which they were asked to implement in order to improve their equal employment and diversity strategies. First of all, Abercrombie & Fitch was legally obliged to establish an office of diversity within the company and to hire a diversity Vice President. Imposing an additional hiring of ten diversity recruiters should ensure a further recruitment of minority applicants. In addition to that, the company was asked to implement special diversity training for its staff, in particular for its management positions. The settlement also includes benchmarks for hiring and employment of minorities. Last but not least, Abercrombie & Fitch was demanded to change its marketing in order to represent a more diverse appearance of its marketing activities (Heinmann, 2014).

3.2 Disability Discrimination claims

In 2009 Riam Dean, a former sales assistant of the fashion chain, took proceedings against Abercrombie & Fitch for disability discrimination. Since a part of her lower arm is missing, Dean has prosthesis, wearing a cardigan in order to cover her prosthetic arm, she was told to work in the stockroom, as she would not fit the company´s Look Policy. The tribunal ruled that Abercrombie & Fitch committed a violation of the employment law since Miss Dean was harassed over her disability (Topping, 2009). Dean was rewarded compensation costs of £9000 (BBC, 2009).

3.3 Religious Discrimination claims

Abercrombie & Fitch was taken to court on account of religious discrimination several times. They were taken to court in 2008 after denying Samatha Elauf a job in a US based shop. The Muslim woman was wearing a black headscarf during her job interview. According to Abercrombie, headscarves do not comply with their Look Policy, as "associates must wear clothing that is consistent with the Abercrombie brand, cannot wear hats or other coverings, and cannot wear clothes that are the colour black" (Hanappi-Egger et al., 2012 p. 228). Arguing that Abercrombie has shown inappropriate hardship by making an exception and failing to accommodate Elauf´s religious beliefs, the fashion chain was found guilty. Elauf was awarded £20,000 in compensatory damages (Liptak, 2015).

4. Current status

Since the settlement in 2004, Abercrombie has undergone changes towards a more diverse image of the brand, which will be discussed in the following part. According to the company´s own information, in 2010, more than 50% of all in-store employees were people of colour (Abercrombie & Fitch, 2010 & 2011). In comparison to 2004, when less than 10% of store associates were coloured, the current number of coloured staff would therefore describe an improvement towards a more diverse picture of the company. However, this number should be treated with caution, as the court-appointed monitor has not confirmed it (Sondak et al., 2014). To comply with the consent decree, Abercrombie & Fitch established an Office of Diversity. Although the consent decree just demanded ten diversity recruiters, 25 were hired in 2005. On top of that, several diversity-training programs were launched.

Although the above developments show that the company´s image towards a more diverse image is in progress, there are also arguments that point to the opposite direction: First of all, referring to the Centre of Equal Opportunities and Opposition to Racism in Belgium, Abercrombie & Fitch has not managed to stop its hiring strategies that favour young, good-looking staff that preferably are under 25 years of age (Danowitz, 2012).

Comparing Abercrombie & Fitch´s intended appearance on its diversity pages´ video with its appearance on its website´s official online store, as well as with its official Facebook page, there is a gap in its diverse appearance. While demonstratively including a lot of employees with different ethnical backgrounds in the video on its diversity page, its official website´s online stores, as well as its Facebook page include, with the exception of one coloured male model, exclusively white, western looking models. Therefore, it could be questioned, whether Abercrombie & Fitch has managed a real change in their marketing to reflect diversity as demanded by the consent decree.

5. Conclusion

Since many of the above stated improvements, which the company proudly presents at its website, were demanded by the settlement, it might be argued that some of its changes simply represent Abercrombie & Fitch´s compliance with the settlement that can be associated with the legal case. Expressing an internally driven organisational self-interest throughout their policy that represents the business-case, it could be concluded that the policy and the reality diverge.

Although they have managed to comply with the law in terms of ethnical issues since 2004, the above stated recent Tribunal Cases show that the clothier still discriminates in terms of disability and religion. This fact underlines the striking difference of the policy and the reality additionally.

To conclude, the fact that the company´s changes towards a higher diversity mostly portrays a consequence to the settlement that is motivated by legal compliance. Thus, the company´s diversity policy, which is argued in terms of the business case, does not seem credible or plausible. Thus, it might be inferred that the policy represents an "empty shell" (Hoque et al., 2004 p.482), as it does contain nothing of substance. It is rather used as "window-dressing" for marketing aims.

In order to bring the policy and the reality closer into line, it should be the company´s highest priority to comply with the law. The failure to comply with the law not only leads to financial penalties, they also lead to a negative image, whilst good practice represents a selling point for organisations (Dickens, as cited in Bach, 2000). Thus, the next stage will be to implement action that supersedes legal demands by credibly celebrating diversity as good practice.

II. References

Abercrombie & Fitch (2010 & 2011) A&F Cares. 2010/2011 Corporate Social Responsibility Report. Available at: http://www.anfcares.org/pdfs/12.19.11%20CR%20REPORT.pdf [Accessed 12 March 2015]

Bach, S. & Sisson, K (2000) *Personnel Management. A comprehensive guide to Theory and Practice*. 3rd ed. Oxford: Blackwell.

BBC (2009) Woman wins clothes store tribunal. *BBC News* [online], 13 August 2009. Available at: http://news.bbc.co.uk/1/hi/england/london/8200140.stm [Accessed 10 March 2015]

Canas, A. K. and Sondak, H. (2014) *Opportunities and challenges of Workplace Diversity. Theory, Cases and Excercises*. 3rd ed. New Jersey: Pearson.

Danowitz, M. A., Hanappi-Egger, E. and Mensi-Klarbach, H. (2012) *Diversity in Organizations. Concepts and Practices*. Hampshire: Palgrave Macmillan.

Edwards, J. (2003) Saving Face. *Business Source Premier*, 44 (36), 16-20

Halasz, R., Swartz, M. and Rhodes, N. (2006) *Abercrombie & Fitch Company*. Available at: http://www.encyclopedia.com/topic/Abercrombie__Fitch_Co.aspx [Accessed 18 March 2015]

Harvey, C. P. and Allards, M. J. (2005) *Understanding and Managing Diversity. Readings, Cases, and Excercises*. 3rd ed. New Jersey: Pearson Prentice Hall.

Heinmann, L. C. and Bernstein, L. (2014) consent decree of Abercrombie´s employment practices. Available at: http://www.afjustice.com [Accessed 10 March 2015]

Hoque, K. and Noon, M. (2004) Equal opportunities policy and practice in Britain. Evaluating the "empty shell" hypothesis *Work, employment and society*. 18 (3), 481-506. London: Sage Publications

Kirton, G. (2010) *The Dynamics of managing diversity: a critical approach*. 3rd ed. Amsterdam: Elsevier/Butterworth-Heinemann

Kumra, S. and Manfredi, S. (2012) *Managing equality and diversity. Theory and Practice*. New York: Oxford University Press.

Liff, S. (1999) Diversity and equal opportunities: room for a constructive compromise? *Human Resource Management Journal*, 9 (1), 65-75.

Liptak, A. (2015): In a Case of Religious Dress, Justices Explore the Obligations of Employers. *New York Times*. 56789 (164), 3-5

McBride, D. A. (2005) *Why I hate Abercrombie & Fitch: Essays on Race and Sexuality*. NYU Press.

McPeake, S (2015) Week 1: A brief history, BMG570 Managing Equality & Diversity. Ulster University, unpublished.

Meisler, A. (2003) When bad things happen to hot brands. *Business Source Premier*, 82 (7), 20

Topping, A (2009) Disabled worker wins case for wrongful dismissal against Abercrombie & Fitch. *The Guardian* [online], 13 August. Available at: http://www.theguardian.com/money/2009/aug/13/abercrombie-fitch-employee-case-damages [Accessed 12 March 2015]

III. Bibliography

Abercrombie & Fitch (2015a) Official Website: Available at:
http://www.abercrombie.co.uk/shop/uk [Accessed 10 March 2015]

Abercrombie & Fitch (2015b) [Facebook]. 12. March. Available at:
https://www.facebook.com/abercrombie?fref=ts [Accessed 12 March 2015]

Abercrombie & Fitch (2012) [video] Diversity & Inclusion at Abercrombie & Fitch. Video.
Available at: http://www.anfcareers.com/page/Diversity [Accessed 15 March]

YOUR KNOWLEDGE HAS VALUE

- We will publish your bachelor's and master's thesis, essays and papers

- Your own eBook and book - sold worldwide in all relevant shops

- Earn money with each sale

Upload your text at www.GRIN.com
and publish for free